TO GET CLEAR

for Sarah, Tristan and Tom

TO GET CLEAR

J. P. Ward

———

POETRY WALES PRESS.
1981

POETRY WALES PRESS
56 PARCAU AVENUE, BRIDGEND, MID GLAMORGAN

ISBN 0 907476 04 X

PRINTED IN 11pt. BASKERVILLE
by
BRIDGEND PRINTING COMPANY LIMITED
TREMAINS ROAD, BRIDGEND, MID GLAMORGAN

*The publisher acknowledges the financial
assistance of the Welsh Arts Council.*

Contents

ACKNOWLEDGEMENTS

Some of these poems first appeared in the following magazines:
Anglo-Welsh Review, Aquarius, Bananas, English, Labrys, Littack, Planet,
Poetry (Chicago), *Poetry Australia, Poetry Review, Poetry Wales, Tribune,*
The Use Of English and *Webster Review* (USA).

Some have appeared in the *Anvil Chess Anthology, Poetry Dimension VI,*
the Welsh anthologies *Green Horse, Poems '76* and *Triangle,* and on BBC
Radio 3 and BBC Radio Wales. 'Before Experience' appeared as a
Sceptre Press Broadsheet.

On The Lake

And he sat, silent as water,
in the stern, a bare rug on his
knees, and a dead perch on the
thwart, dark hills a circling
audience for the fish's eye,
staring up, at the night's expanse
above, and at hills, and a tiny
village and Post Office black on
the shore, and he drew his oars
from the water with no sound, the
blades' flat surface themselves
wet pools, and the lake's
tremendous tilt, to the naked
hills, and he eased another fish,
from the rod's barb, and it
glimmered, and at that moment, he
flicked his rod, from behind him,
and it went up, and the apex of
its cast, touched the North Star,
then fell, past Sirius, past the
meeting of black sky and hills,
sliced into two a farmhouse and
its milking-sheds, sliced down
through clumps of deciduous trees
and oaks, and a stone well, into
the lake, and the rod's needle-
point, pricked the water's surface,
and he waited, and rowed a
silent stroke, and three drops fell
from the oars' arms, and lay like
tiny lakes on the gunwales, and the
rollocks' joints squelched, and he
waited, and he and the hills and
the level lake, passed the night,
while on those hills' further side,
another one lay, a smaller silver
tree-lined lake, staring up from
the hills' timber, like a fish's eye.

Bristol Channel

(Meditation and water are wedded forever.—Melville)

Or any coast . . . Miles out a white
Wave rolls in the distance like a whale's
Belly showing. A single tip
Of white vanishes like a far ship
Going down. There are nicks and falls
Of white so far out at sea they seem
No more than notion or idea of foam,
A nail-paring. A pale hand seems to wave
Then fade, like a riding-lamp seems to give
One beam then not be, a lace
Curtain's corner falls back into place.

Another wave's a sheet laundering.
One like a bar extends its length
And not alone. Through binoculars
Its folding follower jumps in close.
Seen nakedly, small again, but coming.
The next seems like the first's new try.
I'd look for ever, as out there an eye
Does at me, each wave making
New sense, breaking yet not exactly breaking
And soothing the weak sand's brow because
Wave's work is rough as no man's is.

Men once thought it was horses out there
Or a voice singing. You could say so.
Now I cognize a watery shape
Of horse as made by Proteus' deep
And primal as any white-tipped mare.
Beyond, Homer's highway of fishy fins
Up and down channel in sixteen lanes
Permits such legend, cutting across
The tide's direction, drilling its course
Sending wave on wave in just to you,
Thinker. It comes in just for you.

Christmas Day

A wet glove inside-out soon froze.
The neutral copse-gate ledged with white
Seams took on candour. Earlier cars
Left railways with cross-overed tracks
In the snowbound lane. Gunshot and crack
Snapped off when white too much weighed trees
By ice-laced netting where the fruit-
Cage wired fierce jails round raspberries.

Grandchild and son and son's young wife
Shrieked at its silence. 'Look, snow, snow!'
What was this old man's laughing grief
That came? The sky was black, white land.
A photo's negative that damned
All wave-band weathermen had burned
Surprise on their eyes, the children threw
Snow at each other, danced back life . . .

No month, no week can one presume
To live, less still foresee such late
Gift *tabula rasa* like this crumb
Of cut-loaf sparrows might expect,
Hopping with feet a lawn's clear tract,
Day petrified. Two seldom more
Frosts in this glen and temperate
Low-lying dell were wintertime

Each year exceptions none; he'd thought
His past and dazzling Christmases
Dead dreams, and now seized brains forgot
Those yesterdays at this new thing.
Wardrobes of wedding-dresses hung
In the trees, a river's labial cave
Lay flat between white steaming thighs
As though cold thought that wipes growth out

Had more conception than spring had.
The small screen sang: 'And without Him
Was not made anything that was made.'
Could whiteness really make it seem
He'd have a bit more time? Next day
When waking eiderdowned they lay
Watching the ceiling's Dulux gleam,
Sheets slid from roofs, drip-drip it thawed.

Night Sky

We trod a frosty motorway
Unknown to us, no cars passed now
Aphelion's route, ribboned below
A switching-board of stars. I stare
Above, necked cricked, my brain two-thirds
Of one speck on the windscreen.
Quietly there cacks a frightened bird . . .

Orion's elbow dents a hill.
A four-square pane is Pegasus.
Cygnus a delta-wing, its nose
Screaming across to Draco's hole
In the East, the tryon monogram
Of Virgo so immaculate,
Benign, matchless esteem,

No code to crack. Night bleeps and yawns.
They seem to burn intelligence.
Surely they are for something else.
A galaxy's bright chandelier
Depends, apart the Pleiades
A lady's brooch. Rustle
Of ditch is silence. Slight wind is silence.

The Guards

(Augustine: Thou hast made us for Thyself . . .)

We get a stock of bees for food.
I concentrate yet am afraid
Of options gone, there's always been
Distraction. What is that thing
The dark thing certainly not wrong
That holds the centre and from which
All our attentions always switch?

The swarm drops on the laid-out cloth.
A few crawl to the wooden fort
We left, a hive. I watch. Untaught
Then like a moving heap of earth
All take possession of that tang
And waxy place. Then ten weeks from
Their slit the mindless workers come

For pollen masticated crude
For young in each sealed loaded cell.
Then swarm. Invaders are destroyed.
Drones die purged on the landing-sill.
On time in gauntlets and the veil
I sugar where ten thousand live
And take the lid up from the hive.

A detail of the bees swings up
And peels off left to get me; dip,
Savage the gloves, sting leather in
Their suicidal ire and die.
In suit and net and warily
I thieve their honey-frames by hand,
Vats of brown liquid churned like sand.

What do they guard with this fierce work
Vibrating so hard those weak wings
Directing scent? We puff more smoke.
The brood chamber is black as hell.
But who and what you are wee queen
Eludes still, like my childhood, clean
As me decked out in this white shell.

I Do Not Know How To Tell It

I do not know how to tell it
For a reason to come. One morning we
Removed the drone-cells with a knife,
Slicing off those acorn-like protuberances while
The tall ash very gently wavered, forty feet above.
The bees were boisterous but good. We re-assembled
The supers and lifts and then put on the roof.

All day it was hot sun and when I strolled
Along in mid-afternoon my bees
Still flew out at the sky, not settled yet,
Their *pointillist* dots against the brilliant trees.

In the evening I read Maeterlinck on bees: reader,
I did, and for the first time though I had dipped before.
We heard not a sound, not when we put away
Tools or opened a window on the insect-riddled air.

I went then along the greying field to close
The chicken-house. Light was most tricky:
One could see just enough to shut a door.
Then I saw something, as though a bed of cow-parsley
Had sprouted in an hour, four feet high
All round the hive. I went to it. A branch
Two feet thick, almost a trunk, of that ash tree had fallen
Forty feet and missed the hive by a yard.
The enclosure cross-pieces were broken,
The hive itself, between the fork's two branches
Was decked with sprigs of serried ash, the grass
Everywhere strewn with twigs, half-branches, bits
Of lichen-covered wood, firewood for two winters . . .
Had we been there, we would not now be here. I think
Of allegory at the end of allegory. We heard no descent,
In the morning there was nothing, in the night
A massive two-foot weight that would have crushed
A hive's roof or dog's skull and yet did not.

My eyes picked up detail like paint-strokes;
Those countless serried leaves, blades of grass, bits
Of bark, trunks, heads of nettles, a few bees
In front of the hive. We hacked and pulled, broke
And lugged away so the colony's arrival-markers
Could be visible and seen. Tired out we picked up torch
And jackets and went inside. The sky's heat-glow became
More potent in the silence that renewed as we were left
With the last connotation of that day; a hidden level
Hum, as an enormous community in wooden
Walls re-settled for the night.

And how I love the scene
I describe and is our hermitage; small tasks
We do to earn our electricity, that uncoloured
Spirit of the modern world, too lazily disengage
From the sad neurotic hurt, facing rather the clear
Crash of ash on insect's timber and perhaps
Our shoulder-blades or skulls. I see fronds of ash-
Leaf cluster like palms over a swinging
Potentate; I watch my bees, my tiny karate-men,
Lethal Migs, who zoom and ping on my suit's front.

Genes

A duet of boys.
Limbs, sticks of the species
Chubby and spindly knees
No nail yet on their brows.

This fair one is loved
For his forgiving.
I could not do it, have
Such pensive

Clearance in an oval face.
The opal eyes
Accept that he felt no cause
For hurt he willingly allows,

My wood-shaving, my tiny wisp of straw.
Some man years later
May rise from a chair
And tread carpet to you, want you

Astray, his needs to answer.
Then we'll remember
The light on your puzzled hair
My ash-leaf, our sliver of a tree.

Darker, tiny one
What you seem to contain
Is flesh as wit, new-laid comedian.
You looked like a laughing moon

In bouncing back light
Too young to snatch it
Like a ball, to we who pat it.
For your subtler shape we must wait

Then, little egg, fat moonlight.
And if such boys are our contract
In blood, one fair one dark
And both gene mystery, how do we act

Who do not even know
Whence they came, what miracle they imply?
In our eyes prayer
Is impossible, naturally we try.

Winter

I see across the fields a whole
Flock of sheep being rounded up
By a dog. It looks from
Here like a black slug, it lies so
Flat on the snow. Then darts
Through the hedge, a shiny but skilled
Black streak across the white. Then I see
A five-barred gate in front of
Those fields, angular against
Those fields. And there's
The agricultural man, making
Little I dare say from this
Well-fed but tiny flock, yellow-grey
Across the white, the sheet white
Of that field. And if I walk to my cottage
Curving the corner of the hilly
Lane still white with unridden snow, and I
A scholar get back to my room, then I'll
Look out at the snow and then back at
The cool white pages on my
Desk, pages of snow and the
Mysterious black streaks on them.

Fear At Burry Pwll

The biggest trout we took would weigh
Just on a pound. At home we slit
The belly finding eggs, they lay
In pain more than accorded them
It seems, the gut-tied struggling worm
Sure does. And round on history's hook
Are bent men writhing now, the bite
Impends, at least it made me think

Somehow of faults and murky fear.
If we catch fish to recommend
Ourselves as fishermen, aren't we
Just lured there by the trout, mere bait
In dreams of individual might?
Down in the pool you see yourself
And fall in love, we must be drowned,
The screeching reel left by the weir

To have so thoroughly ignored
The long pools of serenity.
We made the needle-points of rod
Inject seed in the river's womb
—Then saw it flick to air like sperm
A dancing eel, figure of eight
Lifting its grey mu-mesons free
To hang up in the moon's strange light

Caught there for man's new study. We
Squirm on the bank, wet alders lean
Their leaves on us, we try to outstare
The circling eddies. We should stock
This stream again perhaps, unlock
More inch-long troutlets into play
Under those same banks where we've seen
Unrescued dead sheep swirled away.

Mud

The stinking clothes delve and exude
Faint chest-hair and are part of him.
Grim blotches on his neck are grime.
I'm spotless from the village shop
At his approach. He flurries me
As black leaves fill the gutters up.

His thumb jerks down to chapel where
They do a dreary tea. Horse-dung
Is parted by my wheels along
The rut between the hedges, we
Its unkempt, tangly hair. A pair
In rank, offensive parity.

This tramp I wouldn't name can't speak.
His mouth has no roof. 'Thas ra Joh'
He splutters, spitting. We drive on,
That voice the unoiled crank you gave
Old cars on frosty days. I beam.
He wipes his nose across his sleeve.

Along the slimy field the sacks
Of spuds sprout up on end in lines
Like dismal churchyards when it rains.
Our clod and vagrant stares with worn-
Out eyes. The shop-girls baby-talk
Him ('Meet me Dai . . . ?'), a dupe stillborn.

He speaks to all the village, just.
He cannot state a thing, or say.
He said fags were his company.
I who utter day and night
For living sense him measuring me.
His tongue your name, my filth, our sweat.

Unusual View Of The Town

No population, roofs that move
Under a slime of rain, and streets
To be assumed, not seen, in spates
Of chimney-pots. A mat of roof
I'd love to walk across and reach
That dismal sea. The ocean's bash
Of waves allures the patent tiles.

No one is ever seen, high up.
And yet I reassure myself
On that, for staring from this shelf
Unites the town and makes its map
Large and affectionate. Roofs lie
Like furrows. Nowhere near as high
As where I stand, gulls scream and dive.

A sense of rest. Banally, beds
Occur to me, under those eaves
And undulating stacks. Are lives
Of consequence in there? Tired heads
In daytime, sex and school of days
Take distant gun-grey waves to erase
Their questioning. Or heal with salt.

I try to hear the indifferent
Long chord of hidden cars. Smoke mists
And wipes and vanishes like ghosts
Of Father Christmas letters burnt
By children, surely dreaming in
Those attics. Daily in dry or rain
The long scene alters. When I climbed

The terraced row above to turn
And stare back down, the roofs appeared
A fraction smaller, like a herd
That moves off timidly or when
A townsman comes. Below, there'd been
Tall gabled windows in between
Sharp gutters. Two more points of view.

The Word-Hoard

When the man died devoid of will
We found his cabinets of print
In the oast-house. They stood arranged
In a tall circle like Stonehenge
Of the big thighs, and one weak light
Low from the cross-beams on a cord
Made tiny shadows down each word
Resetting them. Everything said
Ten billion sentences in lead.

Eight-foot cabinets with drawers
Flat as for maps and seamen's charts.
Damp tried to cool my head and sleeve
This rondel going Aladdin's cave
Awhile. We picked out palpable
Print scattered absently by him,
Our fingers sifting like a dream
In milk if milk's velvet to touch.
I never loved a thing so much.

Every drawer labelled: Spartan Bold,
Bodoni, Goudy, Charlemagne.
Neuland is like the Maltese Cross.
Times serifs tapered like a wine
As delicate as whiskered hair
It nearly moved. Everywhere
Was junk and blocks for Christmas cards
And names and one Madonna and child.
All the texts mirrored in reverse,

Our ultimate talent of mind.
If I were placed to guarantee
My feeble brain's materials,
Writer's materials, they'd be
As weird as this, as mad, the amount
And types of type, small squiggles, tanned
Birds, margins, stars grease-tipped to shine
As though man's knowledge born of print
Regressed from such designing. Wrapped

As we retired I found mint new
The tiniest alphabet, silver
In hue and caught my breath in awe.
A lettered necklace for your love!
How are these icons consummate
In cast so potent? The pen-stroke's curve
Arrested tight grips the word-hoard
Back into rock, then ink from it
Slenders our blood. Some brief small thing

Like 'flesh made word' bears uttering.
And here next week another man
Must re-appear to melt it down
Back to pale lead Bassanio chose,
Winning his tempt. Outside thin rain
Tapping its upright keys on hills
Drops gentle dew from heaven. The best
I take friends and thus in my fist
Hammer-head weights bear down decay.

The Party

And finally the garden and
terrace were finished, and they
decided on a party, with salads, cheese
and a bowl of strawberries, and Peter
and Sue came down the steps with a
bottle of wine and some mushrooms, and
others came, and they had a fat
trestle table, with dinner-plates with
cold meats on, ham, salami, chicken
and some pork, and on an old pub
table beside it, on the lawn edge,
were tomatoes cut into eighths, and
Jim and Hanna came next with their
unmarried aunt, and two or three
groups stood with a fork and paper
napkin in each hand, and a glass of
either red or rosé wine, or tomato
juice, and some had already entered
the cold apple pie, fruit from trees
on the wall, and there was potato
salad, celery, lettuce, and cress from
the stream, and some cold trout, smooth
on the tongue like butter, and all
the eaters stood, not sat, and Frank
was able to pick a rose-petal, and a
whole rose, waist-high, with oil-covered
fingers, where the terrace's slabs
met the lawn, and Shirley spoke to
Martin, handing him a slice of tongue,
and a cold mushroom salad was then
brought out, and shell-fish done with
larger cod in a cheese sauce, and a
child played on the terrace's slabs
with a wheel, looking like a radish
or two, and the apple pie's crust went
slowly up and down, and the juice made
it soggy, and cream licked it, and a
lean dapper man pushed two sardines

with his fork, and with a cube of
bread in its oil, and Donald and Diana
came late, were uncertain but gave a
cask of ginger, and they finished some
uncut cucumber, tomatoes and lettuces,
and very crusty bread before the one
plum pie as well as the three apple
pies, and by then the men were in
threes talking, the girls eating savoury
biscuits and cheese also with the men,
both in some cases, and the champagne
was in some cases, and George put his
plate of Camembert and Brie, and
strawberries, down on the terrace's
slabs for a minute, smiling to the
child to avoid it, and gave Jane some
more cream and red wine in a glass like
a tulip, and there were three red
tulips actually, at the slab's edge, and
I made this into a poem, for poetry is
a necessity, as is food.

The Common Room

This mock-gothic room is bare
At 3 p.m., two weeks before
Our jangling boisterous Christmas Day.
I pass ten minutes' Christmas here.
No books or journals; coffee tables
With no cups, all cleared away
To sud in aluminium sinks
Three doors along the corridor.
A tall unlighted Christmas tree
Decorated with red balls
And silver stuff should blaze the wall
Yet unlighted is bare, seems bare.
White sunlight angles through tall panes
On to the G-plan furniture
They bought for this high-ceilinged room
When glasses on a silver tray,
The velvet sofas, pianos, chests
Of this last-century magnate's house
Were sold to flatter academe.
Christmas comes but once a year.
Mine lasts ten minutes as I sit
Since this room's mien and with no noise
Upends the warm provincial past
Most aptly. Where is everyone?
Vast marble fireplace is a tomb.
Curved mantlepiece a lady's corpse.
False logs ignited by a switch.
Outside a birdless, gravel path
A cold clear air, yet lacking snow.
Ten minutes' fit between the stamp
Of last night's party, glasses thrown
And meetings scheduled for today
At tea-time; something is stopped;
No action, something is still.
A small lacuna once a year,

A plain man's existential rite
In winter, brief, unflinching; cold
December sun affirms us all.
Sun on the faded pastel wall.
Learning is the evergreen.

BP Llandarcy

Blue, olive, pink, buff, chocolate-brown.
A railway train of cottages.

Black crows flap past a wrecked car.
Sheep graze in precious space.

The bare chapel preserves its shape.
No chimney or aerial, just its shape.

Ma scrubs and scrubs, a child recoils.
Dogs fight in the washing-line.

Beyond, on a hilltop:
Two colossal kilns, a pilot flame
And storage tanks settling from the sky
Like flying saucers; pylons as priests.
A chimney points smoke vertically
Sacrificing minerals with uplifted hands.

Each era's fiction, ends up on the hill.
We breathe its silt and sediment.

Search For *Y Gadair Ddu*

(after a lecture on the war poets)

"The attack was timed to commence at ten minutes to four in the morning . . ."

> *(Times History of The War, 1918, XV, pp. 337-9:*
> *"Two Welsh battalions, one of the Welsh*
> *Fusiliers, attacked from the south and south-west,*
> *while another of the Welsh regiments was on*
> *the right of the Fusiliers. More to the*

The chair awaits the lecturer
Who standing lectures. Thane Macbeth
Saw gaps but Banquo's spirit sat
On wood within the mind. Each seat
But one is crammed with audience.
Professors' chairs, Roman *curule,*
Van Gogh's chair pictured with a pipe
On it alone. King Xerxes couched
At Salamis most hurriedly
Jumped up and left, the gold thread gleamed.
The absence sucks the need to know.

> *left of this attack the British Guards moved*
> *to the attack of the defence of Pilkem*
> *from the north of the village. The attack was*
> *made with great vigour, and being of a somewhat*

An empty chair encircled by
The strong crowd watching for a man
To sit on it argues a man
Loved, wanted, but performing first.
So Godot *ex cathedra* makes
No utterance so holds us here.
I never heard of you Hedd Wyn
But for this speaker and *Yr Arwr.*
The cross-kneed ladies scribble fact
In summer skirts so sweet; one must
Say less, one cannot get it all.

28

encircling nature, the Germans found the
Welshman spreading round their flank and
rear, thus threatening their line of retreat.
The artillery barrage guided the men in the

'We have no right to the stars'; not if
We've not lain prone watching the Crab
From four points only victimize sky
Or seen Leo's tail thrashing out life.
Therefore I labour through the books.
They draped the chair at Birkenhead
C Company still sloshing mud
'With skill and resolution' up
The desperate slope to Passchendaele
September out of Zonnebeke.
Each vale of tears wrecks space, shares time.

semi-darkness. At Mackensen Farm they
captured some prisoners and a large store of
ammunition, rockets, Verey lights and
trench mortars. On the left the Welsh

In starts at my researcher's desk
I track him down, both where he came
From but most where he went. I would
Have his existence in myself
—Collapsing myth, or making it?
(Surely they thought he'd send, and with
His Blaenau and Bala chairs; he'd been
A runner-up too? surely some knew
He was dead?) A field-kitchen in France.
At last I find these men, cute, shaven,
Children cut down like swaying corn

Fusiliers, fighting along the south side
of the railway line to Thorout, found some
resistance but captured the 'Zouave House' and
took a few prisoners . . . It was a very heavy defeat

Or soon to be, where splintered trees
Black masquerading like swung men
Caught on this photo as on Keats' urn,
Would gladly stay there but the farm
Is the objective and the ways
Of generals defy all rhyme.
Somewhere far down the reel a man
Collapsed, spun round, or merely lay.
A statue at Trawsfynydd now
Empties its throne and stands stiff, cold:
To this the trail adds nothing more.

> *for the Kaiser's pets.'' ''South of Pilckem a*
> *Prussian Guard Battalion was broken up by Welsh*
> *troops after brief resistance and Pilckem was taken.''*
> *Naval and Military Despatches, 1920; entire report.)*

How fragrant Arras was. Snow like
Black leaves in autumn swirled till noon
In April but this gold watch stuck
Around this exhibition-room
Says seven thirty-six a.m.,
Exactly, sixty years on. Near it
The thin-cheeked, pensive face I'd thought
Was Edward Thomas; it was not,
And ritual chairs retain their ghosts,
Kings, speakers, questioned lecturers
Who've done. By the black trench rest.

> *(9th April: British offensive opens at Arras.*
> *9th April: 2nd Lieutenant E. Thomas, 244 Siege Battery,*
> *Royal Garrison Artillery, killed at Arras.*
>
> *31st July: First day of the three-month battle of*
> *Passchendaele.*
> *31st July: Private E. H. Evans 6117, C Company, 15th*
> *Battalion Royal Welsh Fusiliers, killed at*
> *Pilkem.)*

Notes:

Y Gadair Ddu—The Black Chair. When the winner of the 1917 National Eisteddfod (Birkenhead) Chair competition for the best awdl on the subject Yr Arwr—The Hero— failed to respond to the trumpet's traditional summons, and was then pronounced killed in France five weeks earlier after posting his poem, the Chair was draped in black and remained empty for the ceremony.

Hedd Wyn (bardic name taken by Ellis Evans) did not win the Chair in his lifetime; he was runner-up the previous year and also won six local Chair competitions.

We have no right to the stars—Alun Llywelyn-Williams' translation of *nid oes gennym hawl ar y ser*, the first line of another of Hedd Wyn's poems, written in France. Alun Llywelyn-Williams gave the lecture referred to in the poem.

By the black trench rest—translation of the line from the englyn elegy to the dead poet by R. Williams Parry (also a National Chair winner): Welsh Outlook, October 1917.

The Despatches were published by HMSO in 1920— Part VIII, p.30. The two different spellings of Pilkem in the two passages are as found in them.

Apart from the notable facial similarity, Edward Thomas and Hedd Wyn both died on the first day of the respective battles, and both reached poetic fame by the particular revelation of a pseudonym after their deaths. Edward Thomas saw exactly six minutes of the two-day battle of Arras. How many hours, or half-hours, Ellis Evans saw of the weeks-long Passchendaele engagement, has eluded me.

Moths

Moths litter panes of glass at night and swing
Their frail lace round the outside bulb. They drop
In tiny death to get that sun and plop
Exhausted on a night-lamp's floor. The wing
Seems almost off it spins so hard, the thing
Dies helplessly. I read that if you flop
A sheet across a line and leave it up
All night a thousand types of insect cling
To it next morning, rich with what we know
Not they themselves. Thus you manipulate
Their movements, but that never can reveal
How they should move, or why when they have flown
Their moth's existence ever was, or what
It thought or meant, or in whose eyes was real.

Chess

The woodmen step and drill across the board
In rows of cautiousness. I love this world
Of formal thought and fireside and pearled
Rook-battlements, and how one can't afford
Queen sacrifices if one's less insured
In skill and guile than he. My knight is curled
Now round behind the centre squares, pawns furled
And woven through his line while his adored
King fianchetto gently breaks that side
Like dry ice slowly melting into floes.
His bishops soon hold both diagonals,
His rook the seventh, my defence is wide,
My whole game lost in barely twenty goes.
My king adds one more to its funerals.

Autumn Trees In The Park

Gold bleeds as though the clerks of sun
Had earned good salary. A weight
Of fallen foliage pans down
On grass in gold bricks. Leaves secrete
The colour of June honey. Black
Ideals and morals (branches) move
Behind them, toughening, a groove
Of mind I'm stuck with, then come back
Half an hour later, just to stare.

And find a formal, slender mood
Across the park arranging stones
Like monuments beneath the wood
As this bent Druids' ring does (bones
Of Celtic tourism). A small
Leaf makes a wet tobacco screw.
A large leaf is a boy's brown shoe.
A jogger splats by. Oak leaves fall
In clefts, distribute salesmen's cards.

To let trees breathe some were cut out
By chain-saws or a hafted axe
Or merely pulled. They're placed about
For evident, past reason. Now each makes
A red-hot globular morass
Split from companions by a gap
Of hazy silence. Further up
Tall sun-rods soothe the banking grass
In glaciers, or a gold ski-run.

These old men smoking seem to think
Autumnally. They mull their pipes.
Clean as a towel, a single pink
And eight-inch sycamore leaf wipes
Their bench, and they ignore; like staid
And fed chameleons they sit,

Matching the trees' declining state
While hard October overhead
Ticks off the minutes, old men's time.

Even the railings flake. Dead
Fall isn't punctured by the noise
Of cars outside, nor's silence shed
By the weird echoings of boys.
It hangs in pale, redoubled calm.
The nerveless, huge, unhustling trees
Are annual integers, they ease
And crave their order round the warm
Sun oak makes and was granted for.

The Fan-Tails

(In Memoriam Y.R., killed February 1976)

White doves assembled arduously
Sweep to a gravel turn
And dove-cote clearing at her calling them.
Flight unexpectedly in air
Arriving in the grain's path-making there.

They hear her calling them.
No air behind them skims
The tiniest ripple on their cream of flight.
Only the voice or sembled
Low-key susurration earns that right.

A brief wait, then they drop
Like chalk from roof then straight into that curve.
As though a lily hurled—or sentences,
As though by sprinkling seed so purposely
One found amazing sentences on a blue sky.

She stands, they shift. At expert
Distance she debars herself. Like snow
Or petal-drift they wait, unsure from her address
How she'll take what they form. Then come,
Ignorant still of their own perfectness.

We think she might climb back perhaps
As stumbled from the car so could return
Dazed, blink unwontedly as though to tell
Us her perplexed perception was itself
A smashed contingency, all fact not miracle.

We cope such ways, a sliver
At a time, dreaming she may return
Who self-effaced, who laughed and schemed
And harrowed sometimes, too tough for herself,
Or not returning has not really gone.

As though by bargaining, a void is left.
Or as from work we snare that shattered blank.
No epitaph tires that gravestone.
No prolix line recalls her.
Whiter than sky the fan-tails come.

To My Wife

(the same occasion)

You are everything to me.
No one writes like that today.
Perhaps it's luck to make away
With such love or I fail to see
The territory we live on, you
The garnered path and avenue.

I ran the car down Cadog's hill.
All the leaves fell, all the birds sang.
Our valley's needle quilt is neat.
All the birds sang, all the leaves fell.
You smiled, wrapped in your overcoat
Meeting the boy. Then the phone rang.

Lately and violently you lost
Your blood companion and dear friend.
We male mix round you in small waves.
No one writes like this today
Bar the regressive in our loves.
O clown I want to give you child.

Rain

Faking how bubbles burst, plush drops
Broke on the terrace. Where the slabs meet
But aren't quite level is a light
Puddling the sky. Reflection then
Like a bust mirror's corner gapes
In stone. A kitten's saucer brims
Out on the grass and white sky swims
Miles down in it, making a well.

Thick floods seep on the fields and on
Our patch, as now, bedraggling much
Like a gone tide. I go to watch
It shimmer in the gaps of trees
There upside-down, a window-pane
Of water's stir. I look through seeing
Out of this place and that way being
It all the more. A refracted self?

What is floods' pleasure? Missing rain,
Rain gone, a sky's card sterilized
For once and our quiet fields surprised
In that they too spread mirrors there.
Back home a thrush ripped by a tune
Of gale out of the box-hedge, leaves.
From our one window in the eaves
I look down at, and love, these floods.

Can I say what I feel then? This
Wet maps our guttered house, our boys,
It sweeps the home-made paths, deploys
Grit sand and mud and is my wife.
I need her candid destinies
Enhancing me with dripping guile.
We fence our patch outside awhile
Wet, seeing gates' hinges oiled with rain.

A Volvo swishes up the road.
The rain pin-pricked the stream before
A million hits in one sharp shower
Were like mosquitoes swarming down
The tarmac. Rain on bits of wood
Is drops on old men's noses. We
All play in it like tramps and see
Each other grin through nature's tears.

Electrically the dark falls down
Rain's wires and it is earthed. I write
In it soaked to my jersey, taut
In rain, in love. Like verse, rain is:
Not cloud alone or climate strewn.
Falling sky-water makes our minds
Feel, not new words, but priceless sounds.
The rain sings on the Mini's roof.

Two Events Near Loyola

The car wound steeply down the hairpin trail
The valley's deep fields hazed with mustard, kale.

We reached a speckled village halfway down
With hovels but a massive church. We should go in.

A tiny wrist pulled at the heavy lock.
The latch moved with a huge, explosive click.

Nothing stirred, except the altar's flame.
Priest and kneeler quivered the godhead's name.

We crossed the square, sun-blazed, a moment after
And found a pipe and from its iron mouth, water.

We wallowed in it, slaked it on our hair,
Wrung out our shirts, spun wet drops through the air.

Not just watch-hands told the time to go.
Seconds later, vast valleys lay below.

London Welsh v. Bridgend

Then I got on the train, very late
at night, Saturday, and lay on the seat,
exhausted, as did the other man
there, a little man, beady-eyed and
with a pointed chin, and he pulled the
blinds down, and we lay, and just about
dozed off when bam! door opened,
in came half a rugby team, enormous
fellows, tipped me off the seat on the
filthy floor, then sat down, singing,
shouting, crashing on each other with
their beer cans, and one sat by the
beady man, running his fingers exquisitely
along the fellow's thigh-bone, through
his trousers, but in only a bawdy
way, friendly even, if you could believe
it, and they roughed, and one
arse in the corridor, undid the fire
extinguisher, soaked us, and another
slammed the door, sat down again, kept
asking me the beady man's name, which
I didn't know, angry now, afraid even,
but decided to be sensible, and got
going, talked, had their beer, and they
got serious to meet me, a most
generous gesture, and a big man, older
than the others, kept deflecting the
attention, of the bawdy one from the
beady one, the bawdy one trying to make
the beady one talk, which he couldn't,
in inhibition, and cringing fear, and I
felt sorry, but leant on the carriage arm,
with them, drinking, singing, yawning, and
hearing about his wife, from one of them,
till, at last, they were quieter, they had
won their match, they had had a good day,
and they dozed off, one on my shoulder, sixteen
stone, snoring loudly, but I finally dozed

off, at the train's rhythm, rattling
through the darkness, and I half-woke,
at times, saw a misty scene, as of Arthur's
knights, assembled, swaying, brief white
faces, then dozed, felt the train stop
in my half-asleep condition, and men get
out, a shrieking porter, and banging doors,
then slept again, and then woke, two
hundred miles from London, they had
all gone, every one, bar the beady one, and I
sat, heavy, soggy, wanting lukewarm tea, and
saw, with my round eye and my mind's eye,
the aftermath of dawn, and the mess of the
twentieth century; the industry, the steel
works and the smelting works, a new day, for
better or worse in our hands, and the
carriage window, filthy, but a filter,
for that streaky, watery, nearly
light-blue, blue.

The M1 Dream

I entered in August at Daventry and felt immediately
myself a mere word in a long, composite message down
co-axial cable or three wires to important
London. It was hot; I, protected, who wear
wool on the skin in summer this day had shirt
alone, unbuttoned, both windows down, yet felt air
like warm water still. Our tin column made South,
at 3 p.m. it darkened, sidelights came on and
main beams. Then rain fell like grapes on the windscreen.
Thunder clocked, I saw nearly nothing, nor dared dash
out a lane; in my puny rain-jewelled mirror cars' and
trucks' lanterns shimmered wetly and I could not place them.
Our three lines were submarine, great motorized fish
coming by me. Yet on the surface the sky's black gods
roared at us, lighting splintered the dislodged air.
A porsche sluicing past close a parabola of water blinded
my side window just as I wound the glass up. An empty
lorry bumped by like a badly-dressed fat man; chains
dangling, boards flapping, spraying the rain's saliva
mannerlessly on us others there. In the Toddington
service station I sat awed, the road under the bridge
hissed and slammed with strewn vehicles, and I re-merged
with a nether tunnel of moving lights approaching the ownerless.
We ignorantly drove; our inevitable course, the scared
ecstasy in it history itself, London our moment, our revolution,
our intellects swaying, passed and being passed,
the dark mindless, the blue signs pleading. A transporter
threatened to tip its load, someone mad as the day's
weather sawed his eighty through the hacking rain as we
pushed on, alone in risk yet with splats and blobs of
friendship as a face smiled at a near-side window.
Faded Jesus walked such water serenely; we drive on it,
terrified gripping the wheel, yet a long way off a radio
mast suddenly appeared, a piece of silk sky
beyond it, and what I had most feared became a benevolent
catastrophe merely of recognition, a sun-shafted sky
and houses; and it was just an August after all.

Mind

(Kant's dream)

Is there a structure of the mind,
An amazing structure? Our choice is,
If mind's a pattern made like this
Then all the motes and beams we're taught
Began immovable. But if
Arriving thoughts or feelings are
Discretionary they come from air
And make of mind a messenger.

Is mind enquiring of itself
Just being then, embodied noun?
The bottom can kicked off the shelf
In food-stores brings the whole lot down.
It means in levelling her frown
You end friend's being literally.
She might as well lie in the hay
And plait her auburn hair all day.

If mind is so, and so is mind,
And each a centrifugal force,
Then in reflection we're contained,
Thought laying blooms on thought's own hearse.
Mind has a natural light I think,
Obstructed like the kitchen sink.
But ease that plug, run water through
And Adam's names rotate and flow.

Body

A slice of bread adorns the plate
Fresh-cut to snowy crumbs. Beside
The marble lies some grey-red meat
As thin as evidence, as good
As apple, rolled and cold to touch
Sustaining but not overmuch.

Tall water by this gentle food
Transparently conditions, bland
Cos lettuces with hearts as hard
As ice contrastingly to hand
Imply the biblical bought loaf
And two fish-fingers gave enough.

Five thousand sampled those, now twice
As many don't, yet round this edge
Of china sits nutritious rice
As though our geography could pledge
All mouths forever wide, world-wide.
Each mouthful is a life denied.

If we could stop the hands and bare
All bodies of their flesh and eat
Conscience in perfect gulps of air
It wouldn't make this fast complete,
Nor impulse-gifts, play, plans or work.
Less still our-milk-and-honey talk.

Melancholia

And I descended some stairs,
and saw a woman, fully clothed,
in small light, a dress of silver
sequins, and a gold belt and tiara,
and I stared, while music played,
and she slowly, angled one knee,
lengthening her foot so that the
toe still met the ground, and undid
the belt, took the tiara off, and I
stared, and she undid buttons at her
throat, her collar, and a zip, at her
side, and the silver dress, fell,
to the floor, so that she wore, now,
gold, silver, round her waist, legs
and hips only, which she caressed,
as I stared, as she undid, the fine
silk on her legs, and arms, peeled
it off, slowly, without provocation,
with a constant smile, and the
band's noise, thoughtfully played,
as she undid, lazily, as though
wearily, the thick necklace, of buttons
and beads, the fat opulences, held it,
between fingers' ends, watching it,
turning slowly, as we were to watch,
and she took off, yet another garment,
a fourth garment, a lemon-silk veil
itself thereto hidden, at which
I stared, leaving herself, her calm
body clad, in two things only, in
which one might swim, lie in the
red-gold sky, and she took off one
thing, and her black nipples were there,
as on black oranges in a cowled sun,
and she took off the other, and that
black triangle was there, the crossroads
of her body, the median of mankind,

which now arched, and curled like a bindweed
or a coiling worm, and she looked at
us, her eye a motionless bead.

Heatwave

The news is bad tonight. The ash
Trees turn and wheel toward the west
With gold light on their hair to meet
The sun's command, this summer. Most
News seems like nothing but the swish
Of cattle's flanks going home for night.

Everything's shut in. The hens, the pig,
Small apples hang an abacus
To count my beating heart. This Wales
Shimmers to darkness, night-time moths
Flick in through unfit frames. I drag
My body stiff from working-clothes.

Dreaming fast, I sit right up
And see barred in the chicken-coop
A fox transfigured, as by light.
Motionless, brush so beautiful,
A monogram against the dark,
And all the family are safe.

What is this pleasure-fear in dreams?
He flies up on my mental screen
As if projected by the moon.
As each community redeems
Friends crowd us, and the fox does too
If we impute to him fox law.

Three Walks

I trudged
On the sea-shore, the waves thinned
Evenly to its edge.

The multitudinous worm-casts
Were static, eddies idled
Round my feet.

The wind flicked a scrap of paper,
A bottle lay half-buried in the sand.

Light evening attended, a
Steamer edged out from behind
The harbour jetty a mile away,
A casual silhouette on the waters,
And I felt the jelly, in my foot's flesh,
Of walking across those waters,
It had a tactile substance,
They were so flat, and so serene was I.

Yet I could not, no skill of faith had I,
Only the certainty, that such an evening
Could soothe the mind like this,
Taking the tensions out of it, and the
Waves' crests becalmed, and I walked home
As dark fell, and splashed in the basins
Of my mind.

Before Experience

We toiled all day
Bare to the waist, sweating
With the rocks for dray.

Bulletins told
Of far-away governments,
Promises, Wall Street oversold.

The waves broke
On the shore and salt-thick
Wood lay uncollected, bespoke.

On the shore
Was object-matter; tarred rope, nets,
Seaweed oiled by different work before.

What did we need? To say
'Our spirits ate, we were the nourishers,
We were not unsustained today.'

I lay later, in bed,
Dreamt of the child and starving man
Dreaming of bread.

Sailing

He went on deck, and the yacht's
blade, dismembered the water, took it apart,
threw up white bubbles of entrail, into
the mast, and the boom swung behind him, as they
changed tack, and the white sky of sail,
flapped taut, and quickly filled, tight with
flung air, and the coaming, was wet
where the lee rail had been under, and the
halyards flapped, but tightened, and the boat's
round bottom, swilled and fell flat again,
and he lay, on his spine, aft of the bowsprit,
the jib-boom above, its cleat all but
nudging him, and he saw only sky, with a
masthead vanishing into it, and a burgee,
up there, and the gaff jaws creaked,
strangling the mast's throat, and they gybed again,
the boom walked across, the bent mainsail
filled, the yacht's wood coaled over, and
by his ear, the jib-sheets rattled
along the horse, and they settled again, and
reached, close-hauled, with a beam wind, which,
suddenly strengthened, thrusting the boat
under a blue sky of puffy clouds, and waves
sluiced on the hatches, the jib clew tore
maddened, the foresail tugged, a mop went over-board,
they took in reefs.

Skies

A cloud behind a second cloud
Seems blocked, but when you keep your eyes
Still too they stir, they keep their size
But change their movement. Cumulus
Was like deep piles of snow, a shroud.
One sky was like an oven's fire
Alight as in a furnace door,

A sun but hidden sufficiently
For the effect. An emptiness
I once saw too one dusk, a chaste
Appearance, wads of fields below
A careless void blanked calmingly
As if air, vapour, mist and light
Were only there for staring at

And all serenities were real.
Some skies are paper pulped, with ink
The spattered rain so you might think
Scrawled attitudes were there, or print.
With cirrus, shreds and feathers peel
In bits of cloud, then it aspires
To stretching thin like telegraph wires.

One time a hard grey weight of sky
Felt low and near as if a hand
Pressed quiet but firm on brains. No wind
Alleviated. Then flicked sun
Slid like a cup of water dry
Behind a cloud. The air was damp.
The one bird's tiny wings were limp.

Down The Moor

(they still run wild on the Gower Peninsula)

One moves, her foal a yard behind
Grazing against the mare. To eat
Is soft embodiment of thought,
Turf's sponge was all their feed. The foal's
Knees look like spindly cotton-reels
And canter cautiously. One had
My apple. Lips, a suction-pad

Collapsed the red lump in its mouth.
Twenty-five horses move as one
Their manes across their backs like brown
Dead bracken, nostrils almond-holed.
I never saw a thing less wild.
They drift like tips of breeze, I wish
My thought came naturally such.

A head like glancing silk is turned,
A girl's hand waving. Flares of gorse
All round the motion of the horse
Blaze it out often, like the day.
One shambles suddenly away
Seeing the car, then pauses with
My pocket in its eyes, the mouth

Shut wetly. When the whole herd leaves
The moorland as the instinct comes
They all go off at different times.
One moves a bit, two more graze, stop
Then follow, then to ground they drop
Their heads most naturally. Barely more
Than thought they move off down the moor.

Platonic Immersion

We leave the chlorine, rub us down
With soap then feel a steaming film
Of sweat so tacky none can dry.
The towel's nap wettens and we learn
Where were invincibility
Desire and pleasure, three in one.
All three broke up the waters' calm.

The good and beautiful and true.
Young men rip towels across their backs
Like stropping down their muscles' wit
And Aqualung exponents view
A friend's refracted silhouette
Frogging the tiles below the blue,
Going at the diving-brick he seeks,

While female athletes rail the side,
Soak each pore and deploy strong breasts
Cleaving their liquid's double bulge.
Tall bodies leave the diving-board,
Feet high behind, legs like a wedge
In scintillating entry. Freud
Who inked our thought's wet in suggests

These third moats are natality.
In this expensive college pool
Not double-scotch-and-splash or gin
But water, laved abundantly
Immediate contacting skin
Makes safe such wallowing and free.
As more bath empties, we slake still.

A last wet body climbs out, dried.
Closure of *balneae* of Rome.
Blue racing-lanes calm down and deep
Waves lilt and lop against the side,
Heave gently like a child asleep,
Its stirring done. We swimmers glide
Outdoors and go our three ways home.

As Spenser Says

(Faerie Queene, Bk III, Canto ii)

Britomart, a lady knight
And out of armour beautiful
And powerful, rough in a fight
As Spenser says, one day was shown
A roundglass by a nurse and full
Face there behind her saw a man

Like in her driving mirror. But
Turning she saw only dark
Appointments of the hall, turned back
She saw his face again, red hair
Strong, looking out at Britomart
Convexly and no passenger

Now, front tyre tread for tread with her.
Who was he? No face that she knew.
Red hair, red curled moustache and eyes
Sad with a strength procured in war
Of certainties. As Spenser says,
Some unknown love-dart pierced her through

So softly, lying in her mind
An egg unnoticed. Nurse thought it
A self-projection, Britomart
Coining some rude red-haired desire
But she unhappy combed out her
Tress of bewilderment and found

She didn't like herself and was
Weak suddenly, in one new thing,
That motorbike man, that red-haired king
Outmatched her being anomalous
Like she till now, and she was sad
At the same loneliness he had.

To Get Clear

I knew, all the rest of my life,
that I had seen it, cumulatively,
because of staying until rested in that
simple place of trees and water, and a house
with willow-pattern plates; and the
black cat came in as I put down this,
and growled, sliding the steel-blue
shine of his black body in and out
like a snake, against the table-leg, and
miaouing, telling me of his adventures
in the garden, and demanding food
peremptorily. So I got up, in my jeans
and with the sleeves pushed up to the
forearm, as the fashion is, and poured
a little milk, which it licked, as
though an ice-cream, as though the milk
had a hard edge of matter, which in
a sense milk does. Matter to us now
is mystery of course, that is where
those thinkers of our new past have
taken us. Matter is so nearly eternal
life, as MacDiarmid said; matter is
mysterious, it speaks to us and is
also what we are. How can that be? How
should we know? And yet we know.
    Walking along the lane, I met a
man, and it was Anselm, returning to
talk to me. He said he had thought,
and thought, as though along a renewed
lane, to thought's end, and that end
is Thou, O Lord Our God. I said it seemed
he had changed the gear of his language
deftly, with his left hand turned
upward; he said it was deliberate,
and that the nettles' points

at the roadside had brushed him as he got out of that car, and goaded him into that understanding.

Here, Home

I got home, very late, and parked the
car, by the hedge, and entered the porch,
and was turning the key, when I heard a
single fox bark, a mile away, and I went
inside, put down my suitcase, and spread
my fingers on the wall to find the light-
switch, and one bulb lit dimly, and the
terrier, lying on the carpet, opened one
eye, after a second's pause, and then, a
little later, he seemed, gradually, to be
moving, and raising himself, on rear legs
only, and then the front, with an effort,
and then walked, extremely slowly, about five
steps, to me, where his nose stopped, barely
a quarter-inch, from my trouser-leg, where
he stood, in a kind of acknowledgement, as
it were, and my fingertips touched his wire
head, and I heard, a very tiny breathing, as
of two small people, perhaps, and at the top,
of the stairs, a bedroom door, half-opened,
yielded a cot, with a still form, what I
knew to be, tousled sheets, and one half of
a small, curly head of hair, exposed, like
an object I perceived, or was expert on,
and a little body, under the sheets, which
went up, and then back, so carefully, and
I walked, still with my overcoat, on, along
the passage, past another bedroom, in which
a bigger boy slept, and a further door,
also, was open, to its bedroom, where a
wife lay, in black pyjamas, asleep, the
face loaded, very full, but pre-empted for
the night, and by her, in the double bed,
was a space, the shape and size of a man,
into which I climbed, fitting it, exactly,
and lay half-asleep, templating it, or would
seem so, to a further fox or man who arrived.